THIS PLANNER

Belongs to:

_____

House Hunting LIST

ADDRESS	PRICE	NOTES

House Hunting LIST

ADDRESS	PRICE	NOTES

House Hunting LIST

ADDRESS	PRICE	NOTES

House Hunting LIST

ADDRESS	PRICE	NOTES

House Hunting LIST

ADDRESS	PRICE	NOTES

House Hunting LIST

ADDRESS	PRICE	NOTES

HOUSE SCORE:

PROPERTY ADDRESS

ASKING PRICE:

PROPERTY TAXES:

LOT SIZE:

PROPERTY SIZE:

FINISH:
- [ ] BRICK
- [ ] STUCCO
- [ ] WOOD
- [ ] SIDING

AGE OF PROPERTY:

NEIGHBORHOOD

DISTANCE TO SCHOOLS:

DISTANCE TO WORK:

PUBLIC TRANSPORTATION:

MEDICAL:

RECREATION:

SHOPPING:

ADDITIONAL INFO:

NOTES:

House Hunting CHECKLIST

DETAILED HOUSE FEATURES:

OF BEDROOMS: # OF BATHROOMS:

BASEMENT: HEATING TYPE:

PROPERTY CHECKLIST:

POOL	☐	BONUS ROOM	☐	**NOTES**
GARAGE	☐	LAUNDRY CHUTE	☐	
FIREPLACE	☐	FENCED YARD	☐	
EN-SUITE	☐	APPLIANCES	☐	
OFFICE	☐	A/C	☐	
DECK	☐	HEAT PUMP	☐	

PARKING	☐	**NOTES**
CLOSETS	☐	
STORAGE	☐	
	☐	
	☐	
	☐	
	☐	
	☐	
	☐	
	☐	
	☐	

HOUSE SCORE:

PROPERTY ADDRESS

ASKING PRICE: PROPERTY TAXES:

LOT SIZE: PROPERTY SIZE:

FINISH: ☐ BRICK   ☐ STUCCO   AGE OF PROPERTY:
         ☐ WOOD   ☐ SIDING

NEIGHBORHOOD

DISTANCE TO SCHOOLS: DISTANCE TO WORK:

PUBLIC TRANSPORTATION: MEDICAL:

RECREATION: SHOPPING:

ADDITIONAL INFO: NOTES:

House Hunting CHECKLIST

DETAILED HOUSE FEATURES:

OF BEDROOMS: # OF BATHROOMS:

....

BASEMENT: HEATING TYPE:

....

PROPERTY CHECKLIST:

POOL	☐	BONUS ROOM	☐	NOTES
GARAGE	☐	LAUNDRY CHUTE	☐	
FIREPLACE	☐	FENCED YARD	☐	
EN-SUITE	☐	APPLIANCES	☐	
OFFICE	☐	A/C	☐	
DECK	☐	HEAT PUMP	☐	

PARKING	☐	NOTES
CLOSETS	☐	
STORAGE	☐	
	☐	
	☐	
	☐	
	☐	
	☐	
	☐	
	☐	

HOUSE SCORE:

PROPERTY ADDRESS

ASKING PRICE: PROPERTY TAXES:

LOT SIZE: PROPERTY SIZE:

FINISH: ☐ BRICK   ☐ STUCCO
           ☐ WOOD   ☐ SIDING   AGE OF PROPERTY:

NEIGHBORHOOD

DISTANCE TO SCHOOLS: DISTANCE TO WORK:

PUBLIC TRANSPORTATION: MEDICAL:

RECREATION: SHOPPING:

ADDITIONAL INFO: NOTES:

House Hunting CHECKLIST

DETAILED HOUSE FEATURES:

OF BEDROOMS: # OF BATHROOMS:

BASEMENT: HEATING TYPE:

PROPERTY CHECKLIST:

				NOTES
POOL	☐	BONUS ROOM	☐	
GARAGE	☐	LAUNDRY CHUTE	☐	
FIREPLACE	☐	FENCED YARD	☐	
EN-SUITE	☐	APPLIANCES	☐	
OFFICE	☐	A/C	☐	
DECK	☐	HEAT PUMP	☐	

		NOTES
PARKING	☐	
CLOSETS	☐	
STORAGE	☐	
	☐	
	☐	
	☐	
	☐	
	☐	
	☐	
	☐	

HOUSE SCORE:

PROPERTY ADDRESS

ASKING PRICE: PROPERTY TAXES:

LOT SIZE: PROPERTY SIZE:

FINISH: ☐ BRICK   ☐ STUCCO
          ☐ WOOD   ☐ SIDING   AGE OF PROPERTY:

NEIGHBORHOOD

DISTANCE TO SCHOOLS: DISTANCE TO WORK:

PUBLIC TRANSPORTATION: MEDICAL:

RECREATION: SHOPPING:

ADDITIONAL INFO: NOTES:

House Hunting CHECKLIST

DETAILED HOUSE FEATURES:

OF BEDROOMS: # OF BATHROOMS:

BASEMENT: HEATING TYPE:

PROPERTY CHECKLIST:

POOL	☐	BONUS ROOM	☐	NOTES
GARAGE	☐	LAUNDRY CHUTE	☐	
FIREPLACE	☐	FENCED YARD	☐	
EN-SUITE	☐	APPLIANCES	☐	
OFFICE	☐	A/C	☐	
DECK	☐	HEAT PUMP	☐	

PARKING	☐	NOTES
CLOSETS	☐	
STORAGE	☐	
	☐	
	☐	
	☐	
	☐	
	☐	
	☐	
	☐	

HOUSE SCORE:

PROPERTY ADDRESS

ASKING PRICE:

PROPERTY TAXES:

LOT SIZE:

PROPERTY SIZE:

FINISH: ☐ BRICK ☐ STUCCO
☐ WOOD ☐ SIDING

AGE OF PROPERTY:

NEIGHBORHOOD

DISTANCE TO SCHOOLS:

DISTANCE TO WORK:

PUBLIC TRANSPORTATION:

MEDICAL:

RECREATION:

SHOPPING:

ADDITIONAL INFO:

NOTES:

House Hunting CHECKLIST

DETAILED HOUSE FEATURES:

OF BEDROOMS: # OF BATHROOMS:

BASEMENT: HEATING TYPE:

PROPERTY CHECKLIST:

POOL	☐	BONUS ROOM	☐	NOTES	
GARAGE	☐	LAUNDRY CHUTE	☐		
FIREPLACE	☐	FENCED YARD	☐		
EN-SUITE	☐	APPLIANCES	☐		
OFFICE	☐	A/C	☐		
DECK	☐	HEAT PUMP	☐		

PARKING	☐	NOTES
CLOSETS	☐	
STORAGE	☐	
	☐	
	☐	
	☐	
	☐	
	☐	
	☐	
	☐	

HOUSE SCORE:

House Hunting CHECKLIST

PROPERTY ADDRESS

ASKING PRICE: PROPERTY TAXES:

LOT SIZE: PROPERTY SIZE:

FINISH: ☐ BRICK   ☐ STUCCO   AGE OF PROPERTY:
           ☐ WOOD   ☐ SIDING

NEIGHBORHOOD

DISTANCE TO SCHOOLS: DISTANCE TO WORK:

PUBLIC TRANSPORTATION: MEDICAL:

RECREATION: SHOPPING:

ADDITIONAL INFO: NOTES:

House Hunting CHECKLIST

DETAILED HOUSE FEATURES:

OF BEDROOMS: # OF BATHROOMS:

BASEMENT: HEATING TYPE:

PROPERTY CHECKLIST:

					NOTES
POOL	☐	BONUS ROOM	☐		
GARAGE	☐	LAUNDRY CHUTE	☐		
FIREPLACE	☐	FENCED YARD	☐		
EN-SUITE	☐	APPLIANCES	☐		
OFFICE	☐	A/C	☐		
DECK	☐	HEAT PUMP	☐		

NOTES

- PARKING ☐
- CLOSETS ☐
- STORAGE ☐
- ☐
- ☐
- ☐
- ☐
- ☐
- ☐
- ☐

HOUSE SCORE:

PROPERTY ADDRESS

ASKING PRICE:

PROPERTY TAXES:

LOT SIZE:

PROPERTY SIZE:

FINISH:
- ☐ BRICK
- ☐ STUCCO
- ☐ WOOD
- ☐ SIDING

AGE OF PROPERTY:

NEIGHBORHOOD

DISTANCE TO SCHOOLS:

DISTANCE TO WORK:

PUBLIC TRANSPORTATION:

MEDICAL:

RECREATION:

SHOPPING:

ADDITIONAL INFO:

NOTES:

House Hunting CHECKLIST

DETAILED HOUSE FEATURES:

OF BEDROOMS: # OF BATHROOMS:

BASEMENT: HEATING TYPE:

PROPERTY CHECKLIST:

				NOTES
POOL	☐	BONUS ROOM	☐	
GARAGE	☐	LAUNDRY CHUTE	☐	
FIREPLACE	☐	FENCED YARD	☐	
EN-SUITE	☐	APPLIANCES	☐	
OFFICE	☐	A/C	☐	
DECK	☐	HEAT PUMP	☐	

		NOTES
PARKING	☐	
CLOSETS	☐	
STORAGE	☐	
	☐	
	☐	
	☐	
	☐	
	☐	
	☐	
	☐	

HOUSE SCORE:

House Hunting **CHECKLIST**

PROPERTY ADDRESS

ASKING PRICE: PROPERTY TAXES:

LOT SIZE: PROPERTY SIZE:

FINISH: ☐ BRICK   ☐ STUCCO
           ☐ WOOD   ☐ SIDING   AGE OF PROPERTY:

NEIGHBORHOOD

DISTANCE TO SCHOOLS: DISTANCE TO WORK:

PUBLIC TRANSPORTATION: MEDICAL:

RECREATION: SHOPPING:

ADDITIONAL INFO: NOTES:

House Hunting
CHECKLIST

DETAILED HOUSE FEATURES:

OF BEDROOMS: # OF BATHROOMS:

BASEMENT: HEATING TYPE:

PROPERTY CHECKLIST:

					NOTES
POOL	☐	BONUS ROOM	☐		
GARAGE	☐	LAUNDRY CHUTE	☐		
FIREPLACE	☐	FENCED YARD	☐		
EN-SUITE	☐	APPLIANCES	☐		
OFFICE	☐	A/C	☐		
DECK	☐	HEAT PUMP	☐		

NOTES

PARKING	☐
CLOSETS	☐
STORAGE	☐
	☐
	☐
	☐
	☐
	☐
	☐

Budget & Expenses

PREVIOUS RESIDENCE

EXPENSES	BUDGET	ACTUAL	DIFFERENCE

NEW RESIDENCE

EXPENSES	BUDGET	ACTUAL	DIFFERENCE

OTHER

EXPENSES	BUDGET	ACTUAL	DIFFERENCE

House Hunting NOTES

House Hunting NOTES

House Hunting NOTES

House Hunting NOTES

House Hunting NOTES

House Hunting NOTES

House Hunting NOTES

Address Information

PREVIOUS ADDRESS:

....

....

....

....

REALTOR:

NAME:	....
AGENCY:	....
PHONE:	....
EMAIL:	....

CLOSING DATE:

DATE:

PREVIOUS ADDRESS:

....

....

....

....

REALTOR:

NAME:	....
AGENCY:	....
PHONE:	....
EMAIL:	....

CLOSING DATE:

DATE:

NOTES & REMINDERS

Important Contacts

CLOSING ATTORNEY

NAME:

ADDRESS:

✉ EMAIL:

📞 PHONE:

MORTGAGE BROKER / COMPANY

NAME:

ADDRESS:

✉ EMAIL:

📞 PHONE:

MOVING COMPANY

NAME:

ADDRESS:

✉ EMAIL:

📞 PHONE:

HOME APPRAISER

NAME:

ADDRESS:

✉ EMAIL:

📞 PHONE:

NOTES & REMINDERS

Important Dates

MONTH:

NOTES & REMINDERS

Property Inspection CHECKLIST

EXTERIOR CONDITION:	GOOD	OK	BAD	NOTES:
EXTERIOR OF PROPERTY				
FRONT DOOR				
PORCH/DECK/PATIO				
DRIVEWAY				
GARAGE DOORS				
OUTDOOR LIGHTING				
PAINT & TRIM				
WINDOWS				
WALKWAY				

ROOF CONDITION:	GOOD	OK	BAD	NOTES:
CHIMNEY				
GUTTERS & DOWNSPOUTS				
SOFITS & FASCIA				
YEAR ROOF WAS REPLACED:				

GARAGE CONDITION:	GOOD	OK	BAD	NOTES:
CEILING				
DOORS				
FLOORS & WALLS				
YEAR DOOR OPENERS WERE REPLACED:				

YARD CONDITION:	GOOD	OK	BAD	NOTES:
DRAINAGE				
FENCES & GATES				
RETAINING WALL				
SPRINKLER SYSTEM				

Property Inspection
CHECKLIST

OTHER IMPORTANT AREAS:	GOOD	OK	BAD	NOTES:
FOUNDATION				
MASONRY VENEERS				
EXTERIOR PAINT				
STORM WINDOWS				
PLUMBING				
ELECTRICAL OUTLETS				
FLOORING IN ROOMS				
WOOD TRIM				
FIREPLACE				

KITCHEN CONDITION:	GOOD	OK	BAD	NOTES:
WORKING EXHAUST FAN				
NO LEAKS IN PIPES				
APPLIANCES OPERATE				
OTHER:				

BATHROOM CONDITION:	GOOD	OK	BAD	NOTES:
PROPER DRAINAGE				
NO LEAKS IN PIPES				
CAULKING IN GOOD SHAPE				
TILES ARE SECURE				

MISC:	GOOD	OK	BAD	NOTES:
SMOKE & CARBON DETECTORS				
STAIRWAY TREADS SOLID				
STAIR HANDRAILS INSTALLED				
OTHER:				
OTHER:				
OTHER:				

To Do: Previous
RESIDENCE

DATE:	MOST IMPORTANT

NOTES:

To Do: New RESIDENCE

MOST IMPORTANT

NOTES:

Important Dates

Month

Notes

Moving Day LIST

OLD RESIDENCE

NEW RESIDENCE

Moving Day LIST

OLD RESIDENCE

NEW RESIDENCE

Moving Day LIST

OLD RESIDENCE

NEW RESIDENCE

Packing Notes

Packing Notes

Packing Notes

Packing Notes

Moving Day PLANNER

6-WEEKS PRIOR

4-WEEKS PRIOR

2-WEEKS PRIOR

Moving Day PLANNER

WEEK OF MOVE

MOVING DAY

NOTES & REMINDERS

Moving Day PLANNER

PRIORITIES

MOVING DAY SCHEDULE

6 AM	
7 AM	
8 AM	
9 AM	
10 AM	
11 AM	
12 PM	
1 PM	
2 PM	
3 PM	
4 PM	
5 PM	
6 PM	
7 PM	
8 PM	
9 PM	
10 PM	
11 PM	
12 AM	

MOVING DAY TO DO LIST

ORGANIZATION

REMINDERS

Moving Day PLANNER

6-WEEKS PRIOR

- [ ] HIRE A MOVING COMPANY
- [ ] KEEP RECEIPTS FOR TAX PURPOSES
- [ ] DETERMINE A BUDGET FOR MOVING EXPENSES
- [ ] ORGANIZE INVENTORY
- [ ] GET PACKING BOXES & LABELS
- [ ] PURGE / GIVE AWAY / SELL UNWANTED ITEMS
- [ ] CREATE AN INVENTORY SHEET OF ITEMS & BOXES
- [ ] RESEARCH SCHOOLS FOR YOUR CHILDREN
- [ ] PLAN A GARAGE SALE TO UNLOAD UNWANTED ITEMS

4-WEEKS PRIOR

- [ ] CONFIRM DATES WITH MOVING COMPANY
- [ ] RESEARCH YOUR NEW COMMUNITY
- [ ] START PACKING BOXES
- [ ] PURCHASE MOVING INSURANCE
- [ ] ORGANIZE FINANCIAL & LEGAL DOCUMENTS IN ONE PLACE
- [ ] FIND SNOW REMOVAL OR LANDSCAPE SERVICE FOR NEW RESIDENCE
- [ ] RESEARCH NEW DOCTOR, DENTIST, VETERNARIAN, ETC

2-WEEKS PRIOR

- [ ] PLAN FOR PET TRANSPORT DURING MOVE
- [ ] SET UP MAIL FORWARDING SERVICE
- [ ] TRANSFER HOMEOWNERS INSURANCE TO NEW RESIDENCE
- [ ] TRANSFER UTILITIES TO NEW RESIDENCE
- [ ] UPDATE YOUR DRIVER'S LICENSE

Moving Box INVENTORY

ROOM: BOX NO: COLOR CODE:

CONTENTS:

ROOM: BOX NO: COLOR CODE:

CONTENTS:

ROOM: BOX NO: COLOR CODE:

CONTENTS:

ROOM: BOX NO: COLOR CODE:

CONTENTS:

Moving Box INVENTORY

ROOM: BOX NO: COLOR CODE:

CONTENTS:

ROOM: BOX NO: COLOR CODE:

CONTENTS:

ROOM: BOX NO: COLOR CODE:

CONTENTS:

ROOM: BOX NO: COLOR CODE:

CONTENTS:

Moving Box INVENTORY

ROOM: BOX NO: COLOR CODE:

CONTENTS:

ROOM: BOX NO: COLOR CODE:

CONTENTS:

ROOM: BOX NO: COLOR CODE:

CONTENTS:

ROOM: BOX NO: COLOR CODE:

CONTENTS:

Moving Box INVENTORY

ROOM: BOX NO: COLOR CODE:

CONTENTS:

ROOM: BOX NO: COLOR CODE:

CONTENTS:

ROOM: BOX NO: COLOR CODE:

CONTENTS:

ROOM: BOX NO: COLOR CODE:

CONTENTS:

Moving Box INVENTORY

ROOM: BOX NO: COLOR CODE:

CONTENTS:

ROOM: BOX NO: COLOR CODE:

CONTENTS:

ROOM: BOX NO: COLOR CODE:

CONTENTS:

ROOM: BOX NO: COLOR CODE:

CONTENTS:

Moving Box INVENTORY

ROOM: BOX NO: COLOR CODE:

CONTENTS:

ROOM: BOX NO: COLOR CODE:

CONTENTS:

ROOM: BOX NO: COLOR CODE:

CONTENTS:

ROOM: BOX NO: COLOR CODE:

CONTENTS:

Moving Box INVENTORY

ROOM: BOX NO: COLOR CODE:

CONTENTS:

ROOM: BOX NO: COLOR CODE:

CONTENTS:

ROOM: BOX NO: COLOR CODE:

CONTENTS:

ROOM: BOX NO: COLOR CODE:

CONTENTS:

Moving Box INVENTORY

ROOM: BOX NO: COLOR CODE:

CONTENTS:

ROOM: BOX NO: COLOR CODE:

CONTENTS:

ROOM: BOX NO: COLOR CODE:

CONTENTS:

ROOM: BOX NO: COLOR CODE:

CONTENTS:

Moving Box INVENTORY

ROOM: BOX NO: COLOR CODE:

CONTENTS:

ROOM: BOX NO: COLOR CODE:

CONTENTS:

ROOM: BOX NO: COLOR CODE:

CONTENTS:

ROOM: BOX NO: COLOR CODE:

CONTENTS:

Moving Box INVENTORY

ROOM: BOX NO: COLOR CODE:

CONTENTS:

ROOM: BOX NO: COLOR CODE:

CONTENTS:

ROOM: BOX NO: COLOR CODE:

CONTENTS:

ROOM: BOX NO: COLOR CODE:

CONTENTS:

Moving Box INVENTORY

ROOM: BOX NO: COLOR CODE:

CONTENTS:

ROOM: BOX NO: COLOR CODE:

CONTENTS:

ROOM: BOX NO: COLOR CODE:

CONTENTS:

ROOM: BOX NO: COLOR CODE:

CONTENTS:

Moving Box INVENTORY

ROOM: BOX NO: COLOR CODE:

CONTENTS:

ROOM: BOX NO: COLOR CODE:

CONTENTS:

ROOM: BOX NO: COLOR CODE:

CONTENTS:

ROOM: BOX NO: COLOR CODE:

CONTENTS:

Moving Box INVENTORY

ROOM: BOX NO: COLOR CODE:

CONTENTS:

ROOM: BOX NO: COLOR CODE:

CONTENTS:

ROOM: BOX NO: COLOR CODE:

CONTENTS:

ROOM: BOX NO: COLOR CODE:

CONTENTS:

Moving Box INVENTORY

ROOM: BOX NO: COLOR CODE:

CONTENTS:

ROOM: BOX NO: COLOR CODE:

CONTENTS:

ROOM: BOX NO: COLOR CODE:

CONTENTS:

ROOM: BOX NO: COLOR CODE:

CONTENTS:

Moving Box INVENTORY

ROOM: BOX NO: COLOR CODE:

CONTENTS:

ROOM: BOX NO: COLOR CODE:

CONTENTS:

ROOM: BOX NO: COLOR CODE:

CONTENTS:

ROOM: BOX NO: COLOR CODE:

CONTENTS:

Moving Box INVENTORY

ROOM: BOX NO: COLOR CODE:

CONTENTS:

ROOM: BOX NO: COLOR CODE:

CONTENTS:

ROOM: BOX NO: COLOR CODE:

CONTENTS:

ROOM: BOX NO: COLOR CODE:

CONTENTS:

Moving Box INVENTORY

ROOM: BOX NO: COLOR CODE:

CONTENTS:

ROOM: BOX NO: COLOR CODE:

CONTENTS:

ROOM: BOX NO: COLOR CODE:

CONTENTS:

ROOM: BOX NO: COLOR CODE:

CONTENTS:

Moving Box INVENTORY

ROOM: BOX NO: COLOR CODE:

CONTENTS:

ROOM: BOX NO: COLOR CODE:

CONTENTS:

ROOM: BOX NO: COLOR CODE:

CONTENTS:

ROOM: BOX NO: COLOR CODE:

CONTENTS:

Moving Box INVENTORY

ROOM: BOX NO: COLOR CODE:

CONTENTS:

ROOM: BOX NO: COLOR CODE:

CONTENTS:

ROOM: BOX NO: COLOR CODE:

CONTENTS:

ROOM: BOX NO: COLOR CODE:

CONTENTS:

Moving Box INVENTORY

ROOM: BOX NO: COLOR CODE:

CONTENTS:

ROOM: BOX NO: COLOR CODE:

CONTENTS:

ROOM: BOX NO: COLOR CODE:

CONTENTS:

ROOM: BOX NO: COLOR CODE:

CONTENTS:

Moving Box INVENTORY

ROOM: BOX NO: COLOR CODE:

CONTENTS:

ROOM: BOX NO: COLOR CODE:

CONTENTS:

ROOM: BOX NO: COLOR CODE:

CONTENTS:

ROOM: BOX NO: COLOR CODE:

CONTENTS:

Moving Box INVENTORY

ROOM: BOX NO: COLOR CODE:

CONTENTS:

ROOM: BOX NO: COLOR CODE:

CONTENTS:

ROOM: BOX NO: COLOR CODE:

CONTENTS:

ROOM: BOX NO: COLOR CODE:

CONTENTS:

Moving Box INVENTORY

ROOM: BOX NO: COLOR CODE:

CONTENTS:

ROOM: BOX NO: COLOR CODE:

CONTENTS:

ROOM: BOX NO: COLOR CODE:

CONTENTS:

ROOM: BOX NO: COLOR CODE:

CONTENTS:

Moving Box INVENTORY

ROOM: BOX NO: COLOR CODE:

CONTENTS:

ROOM: BOX NO: COLOR CODE:

CONTENTS:

ROOM: BOX NO: COLOR CODE:

CONTENTS:

ROOM: BOX NO: COLOR CODE:

CONTENTS:

Moving Box INVENTORY

ROOM: BOX NO: COLOR CODE:

CONTENTS:

ROOM: BOX NO: COLOR CODE:

CONTENTS:

ROOM: BOX NO: COLOR CODE:

CONTENTS:

ROOM: BOX NO: COLOR CODE:

CONTENTS:

Address Change
CHECKLIST

UTILITIES:

ELECTRIC

CABLE/SATELLITE

GAS

SECURITY SYSTEM

PHONE

INTERNET

WATER/SEWER

OTHER

OTHER

OTHER

FINANCIAL:

BANK

CREDIT CARD

BANK STATEMENTS

EMPLOYER

INSURANCE

OTHER

OTHER

OTHER

OTHER

OTHER

New Provider CONTACTS

MEDICAL

FAMILY DOCTOR

NAME:

PHONE:

EMAIL:

ADDRESS:

WEBSITE URL:

DENTIST

NAME:

PHONE:

EMAIL:

ADDRESS:

WEBSITE URL:

PEDIATRICIAN

NAME:

PHONE:

EMAIL:
ADDRESS:

WEBSITE URL:

NOTES

New Provider CONTACTS

EDUCATION

SCHOOL #1:

NAME:

PHONE:

EMAIL:

ADDRESS:

WEBSITE URL:

SCHOOL #2:

NAME:

PHONE:

EMAIL:

ADDRESS:

WEBSITE URL:

SCHOOL #3:

NAME:

PHONE:

EMAIL:

ADDRESS:

WEBSITE URL:

NOTES

Start / Stop UTILITIES

ELECTRIC COMPANY

NAME

PHONE

WEBSITE URL

START DATE

STOP DATE

ACCOUNT NUMBER

CABLE / SATELLITE

NAME

PHONE

WEBSITE URL

START DATE

STOP DATE

ACCOUNT NUMBER

GAS / HEATING COMPANY

NAME

PHONE

WEBSITE URL

START DATE

STOP DATE

ACCOUNT NUMBER

Start / Stop UTILITIES

INTERNET PROVIDER

NAME

PHONE

WEBSITE URL

START DATE

STOP DATE

ACCOUNT NUMBER

SECURITY SYSTEM

NAME

PHONE

WEBSITE URL

START DATE

STOP DATE

ACCOUNT NUMBER

OTHER:

NAME

PHONE

WEBSITE URL

START DATE

STOP DATE

ACCOUNT NUMBER

NOTES:

Room Planner

ROOM:

PAINT COLORS::

COLOR SCHEME:

DÉCOR IDEAS:

FURNITURE IDEAS:

NOTES:

ROOM:

PAINT COLORS::

COLOR SCHEME:

DÉCOR IDEAS:

FURNITURE IDEAS:

NOTES:

Personal NOTES

Personal NOTES

Personal NOTES

Personal NOTES

Personal NOTES

Personal NOTES

Personal NOTES

Personal NOTES

Personal NOTES

Personal NOTES

Personal NOTES

Personal NOTES

Personal NOTES

Personal NOTES

Personal NOTES

Personal NOTES

Personal NOTES

Personal NOTES

Made in the USA
Las Vegas, NV
26 January 2025

16983950R00057